Discovering What to Say

Wally Swist

Bainbridge Island Press

Discovering What to Say

Wally Swist

Bainbridge Island Press

Bainbridge Island, WA

Discovering What to Say
by Wally Swist
Copyright © 2025
All rights reserved

Published in 2025 by Bainbridge Island Press
Bainbridge Island, WA
https://bainbridgeisland.press

Printed in the United States of America

ISBN: 978-1-961451-12-4
Library of Congress Control Number: 2025946604

Cover & Book Design: Ben Rockwood

9 8 7 6 5 4 3 2

For Tevis

Contents

4

Discovering What to Say

Discovering What to Say

for Father Gabriel Rochelle

You write informing me
that you have traced your German surname
back to 1100 in Blaubeuren
and to two brothers who lived *auf die riede*,

or "by the swamp (reeds)."
How much like you
to provide the exegesis and the argument
at once, igniting my memory

of our once-a-week Monday talks
in your book-lined study facing
High Street, the tops of the heads
of passersby moving to and from

classes at the university,
when sometimes the very air itself
would fill with the intensity
of our conversations, the books

I would bring, the authors I would
introduce from my hours working
in the bookstore, and you sharing
the depth of your knowledge

and your active wisdom such as
how people forty thousand year ago
fashioned bone pipes in the caves
near Blaubeuren, how these pipes

were both discovered and their images
reproduced in paintings on the walls,
how you facilitate my hearing
the melodies of their playing

not because they have nothing to say
but exactly because you and I
will always discover what to say
and what is most specific to express

like the fires of an idea
that can even light up the walls
of a cave, just like that evening
I dropped off a Christmas gift

to you of a copy of David Jones'
In Parenthesis, his book-length
poem of fighting in the trenches
in World War I, the snow falling

as slowly as in a paperweight,
and you meeting me at the front door,
the hallway lit behind you, intimating
the length of the decades we would

remain in contact and in friendship,
wherein there have been silences
that are always filled again with words
we needed to say and said them

with clarity, not unlike the residents
of caves who sat beside the flames
of their hearth and blew into
their pipes of bone by discovering

what they had to say, as we have been
trying to leave a trace of the sacred,
so anyone could clearly see it
and begin to listen to it fill the air.

November, Migration

We hear them barking beyond
　　　　the tall crowns of tulip trees above
our heads, as they emerge from
　　　　the edges of the fluttering russet
leaves, the large flock of them,
　　　　exhausted, hoarsely calling, one
after another slowing their flight,
　　　　then circling as a group, an avian
choreography, which brings them
　　　　closer to their reflections moving
along the surface of the pond. How
　　　　they lift their wings, concomitantly,
to lower themselves into
　　　　the water, to drift in free fall, each
one splashing and dragging
　　　　their bodies into the churning spray
they create, each one a susurration
　　　　punctuating the conclusion of their
flight, with a hiss, and their
　　　　mingling honking cries, until they
rest and bob in the waves they
　　　　launched, one by one, and as a flock,
rippling along the shore, enrapt
　　　　in a moment of silence, which washes
over them and ourselves, filling us.
　　　　What it is to see them again, what it is,
with such subtle astonishments,
　　　　for them to have flown and then landed.

Taking Care of the Horses

In Memory of Russel Williams

For three years
you took care of the horses,
and by your becoming
one with the horses
you experienced an awakening
that didn't diminish
in its astonishment and clarity.

For three years
you took care of the horses,
and despite your near drownings,
the electrocutions, your
persevering the ravages of poverty,
you survived to break through
into the constancy of being one

with everything. Beginning
with being challenged by
a trainer in the circus who
couldn't handle the most
temperamental horse, but you
looked into his eyes, calmly
slackened the rope then led him

around the ring in a slow trot,
further grooming and feeding
the horses, and whispering into
their ears, not thinking about
yesterday or tomorrow, but just
being in the moment with them,
the expansion of which rippled

like water over a still pond,
or the way a horse's skin shudders

8

when they experience delight
or joy, or pleasure, or when
your eyes and theirs met,
and the very air between you
was electrified with your presence
and theirs in a union in which
the essence of being alive
rippled in you and them,
not in tension but in knowing
they were you and you were them,
that there was no difference
and nothing between you

other than what is sacred, what is
divine, and that is why the horses
loved you and you loved the horses,
why you forgot the parameters
of your own body and mind
and each transcended and trusted
the other, their hoofs echoing

around the hard-packed dirt
of the ring and circling the paddock,
the horses whisking their tails,
flouncing their heads, and neighing
as they pranced beside you, and you
connected with them as much as they
were connected to you and not you,

as you would later write in Not I,
Not Other than I, advancing further
in the concluding chapter how you
were aware of the realms celestial
being present with others in the room,
how benevolent nothingness was, how
we can merge with that and hover there.

After the Blizzard

The fox prints puncturing the surface
of the snow after the blizzard
score its whiteness—
the same four notes pressing themselves
over and over again, in a meandering line
across a page, that is more silence
than music, but is still a melody that
can barely be heard,
shadows filling the tracks beneath
the pine branches shifting in the wind.

But it is the sound of the bells
that not so much startles me
as it offers me solace, ringing
from a distance, this soft chiming of sleigh
bells, until as it gets closer, it is more
of a whistle, the notes becoming distinct—
making me aware of its velocity, now
in flight, the tinkling call of a white-throated
sparrow, streaking close to my ear, melding
its voice with the streaming winter sunlight.

Carrying the Stone Buddha

I could tell by the hush
even walking down the back stairs
that it could have fallen overnight.
It wasn't until you opened
one of the blinds that we saw

its whiteness, that initial surprise
covering the ground
with its freshness, giving the blank
emptiness of the cold a form,
even a sublime beauty. Just

the first snow dusting the surfaces
of everything gave it an omnipotence
however brief, since it would
melt in the sun, as I swept it
off the driveway and porches

with a broom, but it was my walking
through it, actually my trudging
along the accumulation of it, giving
it heft, carrying the stone buddha
you had wanted placed beneath

the enormous pine in the backyard
by the windbreak, that I became
aware of the significance of the act
itself, and the realization it brought,
that as vital as its falling

and having fallen, and as alive
in the moment we might be,
carrying the stone buddha, all of us,
and everything, returns, always
to the silence from which we came.

Golden at the Trough

You look as though you could
tip the bowl and its contents over,
clutching one end of it with

your yellow talons, staring into
the reflection of sky
in the water. Philosopher, shaman,

spirit king, weighty presence
of astonishment, peering into
the trough's turbid pool,

mourning the mate we saw you with
last year, no longer to be seen,
all two feet and more of you

from head to tail tip, your dark
feathers a mystery, and those
deep brown pinions alerting us to

your name. You survey the land
then look back at the reflection
in the basin beneath you.

Your spirit inhabits the wiry strength
of your body, your wings,
those unrelenting and unforgiving eyes.

When I step quietly onto the back porch
that is too close and not quietly enough,
you push off and up into your brethren,

the air, your white leg feathers and bib
flashing before you land in the birch
in the tree break, where you begin

your keening again, then a moment
later disappear somewhere far beyond
my capacity for attention. How you wear
your name with utmost humility,
the way those dark brown feathers
only accentuate the black ones,

keeping us guessing and in awe,
golden eagle, bird of sorrow and grandeur,
shapeshifter and lamenter, the sharpness

of your cry catches me within, the breadth
of your wings fills me, the haunted
look in your eyes remains in mine.

Black Bear Cub Crossing the Road

It startled us by stopping
on the gravel beside the road,
sunlight bristling on its coat,
understanding we must have
startled it by it having startled us.

It lingered a full moment,
giving us the opportunity to assess
that despite the luster of its fur,
it was underweight, most likely
due to the drought

browning the undergrowth,
but the cub's cautious hesitation
was part of its innate grace,
intuiting the time
that was apt to plunge forward

again, all four paws in rhythm
of a quick stride, a gait
that it appeared to float upon,
effortless, but determined,
perhaps making up for lost time,

knowingly entering the woods
on the other side of the road,
perhaps picking up the scent
of its mother, or its brethren,
passing desiccated berries

it once gorged on before the rains
stopped falling, loping past
dried hobblebush and chokecherry,
a dark streak in the dappled
sunlight, crunching over leaf litter,

snapping fallen branches, in pursuit
to finding the way to one den
or another, parched, as we became,
in observing it taking flight, as it had
observed us in our catching sight of it.

Green Heron

What counterpoint
to such inherent stillness
but the ripples

lengthening themselves,
moving toward
the shore just behind you.

The colored leaves
mirrored in the water that
you stand above,

as if you aren't even there,
but how present you are—
you with your silver wings

tucked in over your legs,
two stilts that hold
your quiet elegance aloft.

The green patch atop
your head, a crown attesting
to your watery life

devoted to the art of fishing,
of honing your craft
of the catch, making it nearly

indiscernible, marking your
quickness, agility in motion.
How you mesmerize those

who are fortunate enough to
find you transcending
your surroundings for one

pure aim: to sustain yourself;
as we nourish ourselves
in watching you reflect on

the stillness within,
the transformation of that
without, remaining true

to your nature, green heron,
making us look deeply
within ourselves,

so that we might recognize
what is intrinsic within
the harmony without.

Redtail atop the Larch

How you shake out your broad wings,
cleansing them in the rain, how you keep
spreading those pinions with the storm

still beating down on you atop
the enormous larch, whose crooked crown
points skyward, all the while you release

your hoarse cry into the lashing wind
and rain, losing your footing on a branch,
then regaining your perch with the vice grip

of your talons, undulating your wings
again, washing away whatever it is
you are trying to clean, possibly oil from

the cove at the marina, cleansing
and cleansing each of those chocolate-brown
wings and shaking them off, as a taunt

or in a fury, over and over again in
expressive heaves and ripples of your body
atop the larch, making the racks of the highest

branches rock in the rain and the wind,
with you as avatar, an emissary of the divine,
in shaking your heavy wet feathers,

by just unleashing the wildness from
within you, from your aerie, pivoting
from one branch to another to continue

to cleanse those wings you raise in the air
one at a time, the rain falling harder
and harder to the rhythm of your dance.

2

This Morning

— Sono Mama: "Just as it is"

The aromatic sweetness
   of the thicket wild with
      fleabane and milkweed

opening into fragrance,
   where two deer
      must have strode

through those tall stems,
   knocking some down,
      creating new paths

from which
   the redolence emanates
      even in the slightest wind,

is nearly overwhelming;
   the call of a cranky catbird
      wrenches its sound

all the way down
   beyond the slope of the knoll,
      where the grove of trees

stops before the sky and all
   the passing clouds that are
      held in the pond's mirror.

Button Box

The round tin
that once contained
the holiday rum cake
which was always shifting
with a festive load
of my mother's buttons—

varieties and sizes
of deep rich colors:
chocolate browns,
pomegranate reds,
sporty dark blues,
all of them sliding over

each other at just the touch,
making a rushing sound.
Sometimes the silver surface
at the bottom flashing
so that it became a mirror,
and you could see yourself,

momentarily, surprised
to seem so avid in your delight.
I remember placing my hands
amid the buttons
and allowing them to stream
through my fingers

one after the other,
feeling the satisfaction
of their diversity,
their utility, their charm,
and trying to guess
which one might be used next—

to be sewn onto
a sleeve, or attached
to a collar, or added
to a winter coat: the deep greens,
the azures, the pearls.
To be able to reach in

and hold them
while my mother sewed,
calculating where they might go
took up some of the best,
and most hallowed,
of my boyhood hours.

Creche

The word itself when spoken
      is the sound of straw shifting among
its innumerable strands,
      in a whisper; a hush, when pressed,
or laid amid, or sat upon,
      which was also the sound of tissue I
unwrapped from the ceramic
      figures: Mary, Joseph, the three wise
men, a donkey, some lambs,
      the Christ child, wrapped in swaddling,
laid in a manger. The figures
      were packed within an open barn stall
with a thatched roof, and it was
      fragrant with the scent of the previous
Christmas bayberry   candles,
      the ones mother burned before her death,
Christmas also being her birthday.
      How reverently I held and then arranged
each figurine, placing each in
      a circle surrounding the manger. There
were even figures of angels
      which held trumpets that I placed on top
of the roof, announcing their
      clarion sennet in my imagination; but
it was the pronounced silence,
      the stillness inherent in the character of
each of the figurines that transported
      me to not only the birth of Christ but also
to recalling my mother, her essence
      levitating amid the tableau, something of
her barely discernable within
      spaces between figurines themselves, and
the softness of saying the word
      creche, as I whispered it, that made me

believe there was something that
       hovered in the air there, quite eager to
return my perception amid
       the nothingness that perpetuated such
wonder emanating in the silence.

Angelic Numbers

111

Influential for manifestation.
Make a wish when you see it
repeated in a sequence, as in
11:11. Pay attention to
your mind; all dreams, goals,
visions can be replicated.
Focus your energy on ushering
any and all positive intent into
the essence of your existence.

222

It's never proactive to compare
yourself to others. Don't be
concerned about being at
a particular point in your life.
Angels want you to remember
the importance of not only
being present but also savoring
the moment, knowing you are
where you are supposed to be.

333

If you're needing more balance
living your life, you'll see this
prompt. Angels will remind you
that you need to adapt, reimagine,
recalibrate. Don't procrastinate.
You're not self-fulfilled. It's time to
engage with yourself as well as others,
to embark on a journey, as Rilke
suggests, "you must change your life."

444

During times of struggle, this number
indicates there'll be signs, a spirit
will come to guide. Consider this
numerical sequence evidence that
you're being heard, that perhaps
a multitude of angels are answering
the prayers you release to protect you,
that they're on their way. It might be
a colossal battle, but you'll be led to light.

555

If you start seeing this repetition,
be prepared for coming change.
Difficult or not, it's your time to
readjust to the positive, revise
your purpose, take matters at hand
differently, lean into what's proactive,
align yourself through assistance from
your angel, when that's done, there'll
be a difference in getting what you want.

666

Scrooge may have seen this
succession of sixes before recanting
his ways. If you see it, know that
your angel is attempting to get
your attention. It's an emphatic
message. Ask yourself what
you need to do differently. It's time
to get a hold of your life. Take
responsibility. You need a life review.

777

Recurring sevens such as these
are a sign that the divine is urging you
to let go, relinquish your fears,
listen to Doris Day's advice, *Que Sera,
Sera*. No worries. What will happen
next happens next. Be one with
the present. Have trust in all that
is working for you, know that at this
particular moment it's all working out.

888

Revolving eights portend. Perpetual
energy figures itself around you
in loops. Think infinity, although
you think that can't be done. Be open
for what is effortless, the astonishment
of grace you have to look forward to.
Think natural flow. Feel its rhythm.
It's not if but when you feel that pat
on the back, practice active gratitude.

999

What's fine about this number is
the loveliness of replicating nines.
Dante said Beatrice was a nine,
her beauty was so complete. Nine
cycling through your life intimates
realization. You're about to achieve
objectives, ascend the mountain, break
the tape at the finish. Smell the roses
but it's time to climb another peak.

An Offering of Grace

In memory of Linda Gregg

She appeared to me in the dream,
white frock flowing,
her hair shining, as if she had just
brushed it a hundred times,
as she often said she did;

and it was the sweetness
in which she could offer kindness
that could level most hardships
in an abatement, an assuagement,
which was an offering of grace,

until she morphed, as she
explained to me in the dream,
into all of these other selves,
younger versions of her, until
in the youngest I could only

last see her luminous eyes before
she disappeared when I awoke.
Her tone reminded me
of when we were at the gathering
after her talk on Dickinson,

and we were with Jack beside
the catered table when she mentioned
to us to wait there while
she would fill our plates for us,
and later she would fill her own plate

upon which she would return
to the conversation. Linda, always
intuitively in touch with the depths
of the power of her femininity,
resilient in herself and reaching out

to nurture others for whom she cared,
not unlike when she appeared to me
in the dream, rejoining me
to not only the best route but also
even the only route, despite

disappointments and distractions
to harvest the honey from the combs,
which, as she enumerated
by revelation, if you only remain
open to sustenance and nurture,

just continue to flow and flow.

Looking at Putin

"He is small and pale . . . so cold he is almost reptilian."
—Madeleine Albright, Former Secretary of State

Looking at you,
the ice frozen forever in your heart
dislodges as you clench
and unclench your fists—
the block of it beating against
your aortic walls,
similarly as you must have beaten
false confessions out of your captives
when you were in the KGB.

Looking at you,
I imagine a dissonant balalaika
strumming inside your perilous mind,
one which never knows
a moral imperative but choses
instead the path to power
by any means, and whose method
no matter how patient you may seem
can be described as breakneck speed.

Looking at you,
I consider what Pasternak would have
thought about what you are, how
he would have assessed your levels
of darkness, and acceded that
your active malevolence and simmering
hatred are bleaker than any Russian
winter, wretched enough to wither any
windowpane of Zhivago's frost flowers.

Looking at you,
I see the discomfort you might feel,
if you feel at all, at having such
inhumanity packed into what appears
to be a human body; although

even your skin doesn't seem to be
soft as flesh is, but made of cartilage
as sharkskin, as if we could peal
that away and there would be,

looking at us,
another Putin, one smaller than
before, each a Matroyshka doll packed
within another, but yet one more
Putin, the evil spreading countless
ways, which proliferates with such
maliciousness as with all of the little
windup Trumps that we now see
muscling in to overtake our world.

Manacled

The image, in Bucha,
of the dead man's hands
bound behind him, is all
we need to know of barbarism,
the nails of his fingers
as gray as the gunmetal sky,
under which he was murdered.

To deepen the offense
Russian aggressors accuse
the Ukrainians as being the Nazis,
rubbing the proverbial salt
into the wounds of their victims,
obfuscating the truth with lies
as they try to wipe their hands

of the genocidal blood.
In Bucha, we see this man's hands
bound behind him in a mass grave,
among his neighbors,
among those whose hands
are also bound, some raped,
executed, slaughtered

as one Russian intellectual
advocated: to clean Ukraine,
to make pure again,—
which makes for a totalitarian motto
for the new Nazism rearing
its depraved head
from its pseudo-proletarian czar,

Vladimir Putin, the embodiment
of evil, scourge walking
the face of the earth,
making this a war between
what is corrupt and what is noble,
exemplified in
the manacled hands.

Blue Evening: for Doug Brown

blue stream flowing gently over our heads

—an unattributed quote from Novalis,
from Penelope Fitzgerald's Novel, The Beginning of Spring

You stood out
like the flute solo in Mendelsohn's
Reformation Symphony, which
was actually his second and not
his fifth. You stood out:
bright yellow hair, sensitive lips,

your eyes an intense blue.
I was honored when
you chose to room with me,
share the third floor flat
on Lake Place behind
the Payne Whitney Gym.

I will always be grateful that
you did so because you trusted me.
People raised their eyebrows
and spoke in whispers when they
learned about your I.Q.
As a philosophy major,

in your freshman year, one
of your instructors thought so highly
of a paper you had written
they had it published in an academic
journal, despite it not being typed
but written in your illegible hand.

You never made it past
second semester, and there were
scars that marked each attempt

like permanent welts on each
of your wrists. I will always be
appreciative of your recommending

Novalis, the German poet-philosopher,
his *Hymns to the Night,* which
inspired Penelope Fitzgerald's
masterpiece, *The Blue Flower,*
but we still drifted away: my going on
to take a job in another bookstore,

you staying on to take further comfort
in what was rote. Our bond
was one of quietude, our appreciation
of the sublime. The last meeting
was by serendipity, as was our first,
when we were both about to leave

New Haven, walking into each other
on Trumbull Street, in front
of the rows of brownstones, you relaying
that you were giving up trying
for a degree, to play it safe by taking
an administrative job your father had

arranged back in West Virginia.
I shared that my plans were to try
to make a new home in Massachusetts.
You assuaged me that whatever it was
I did that I would make it, but you
were much more uncertain

about how you might do, twilight
backlighting the dome of Woolsey Hall
in the near distance, into which
we turned to walk beneath a sky of high
clouds, and under which we departed

through a winter evening's early blue.

Sam Murray, Bookseller

In the late 40s, after the war,
your territory representing Rand McNally
stretched from western Pennsylvania
to Maine, and all along the way
you stopped at every used bookstore,
come to know every book dealer,
selectively accruing local histories,
fine bindings, Limited Editions Club
classics in slipcases, and your reference
of books on books, which I would see
sitting in your study, as we politely
parleyed the cost of each book
I selected for my bookstore's stock
because you purposefully neglected
to place a price on them.

           Your reference
library stretched in splendor
from floor to ceiling, shelf after shelf
of bibliographies and auction records,
where I would sit on the floor
at your feet, venerable Scotsman,
wise and kind heart, never quite making
my turn in profit that was the norm, but
acquiring clean copies of rare books
that sold right after I brought them into
the store. Always remembering
your wife's insistence to stay for lunch,
simple fare tasted more like haute cuisine,
Campbell's tomato soup

                              and tuna fish
on white bread, in that grand dining room,
the three of us sitting in the ambiance
of a painting by Norman Rockwell,
always the quality of the light slanting
through the windows a remembrancer
of a prospective on a palatable eternity
amenable and welcome for all, not unlike
your sharing your perennial philosophy
after the penultimate heart attack, with you
comfortable again, lounging in your robe,
as we gently haggled over the prices of books
in the stacks I had culled from your shelves,
and you offered that *life was like a layered
box of chocolates,*

                              and you had thought
that there were none left
on what you had surmised was the last layer,
until you discovered you could pull back
the fancy dark cardboard separator
and you found an entire layer more to enjoy,
the spines of the books lining the shelves
from ceiling to floor shining their tributes
in the lamplight, their raised spines and gilt
lettering radiant and gleaming,
never a moment of ultimate despair apparent
in your voice, always that glimmer in your eyes,
the sparkle in your wry smile, your swivel chair
squeaking with a renewed joy with your weight,
that now is your legacy to me through
the decades of what a bookish life can emulate.

Finding the River Within
For Duane Whitehead

1.

English colonists called the town Great Falls
but the translation of the original Abenaki name

for waterfall is *Kitchee pontegu*. The first bridge
over the Connecticut River, built in 1785,

the Arch Bridge, was replaced by
the New Arch Bridge, in 1903, and the factories

there produced iron castings, carriages, shoe pegs,
and organs, hence the name, Bellows Falls.

2.

You quote Carl Sagan, "inquiring minds need to know,"
exemplary of your being proprietor

of Arch Bridge Bookshop on Village Square,
connecting prospective readers with pertinent books

to fit their interests. As one browser says, "Like walking
into a time warp." Another compares the bookshop

to The Strand, in New York City, but stresses that it is
"less organized" but "has a similar vibe," that they "loved it."

3.

You are not only a man of ideas, but you also have a passion
for discussing beliefs and plumbing information for facts,

espousing ancient history and the Battle of Thermopylae,
recounting what the Persian Xerxes sought to accomplish,

how the Spartan Leonidas won out in the sea battle
at Salamis, how you inflect in telling the story that

it is an example of a smaller force defeating a larger one,
that what was saved was all of western civilization.

4.

When you ask me about what it means for me
in finding the river I summon the journey of discovering

the heart, what draws us up into the center of our lives,
what moves us forward, what currents flow deeply below,

and I see you nod your head in agreement, having already
been a seeker of wisdom, exemplifying the way Thoreau

imparted the one mile climb to Table Rock on Fall Mountain
was a destination where one could consider the flow of the river.

Good Buddhism

for William Ackerman

We'd see you always seated
next to your accompanist,
Saturdays, late morning,
in front of the music store
at the bottom of Main Street
in Brattleboro, but it was you,

wearing the fingerless gloves
those winter days, how you made
the notes bounce off the red brick
buildings on either side of the street,
with the purposeful and slow
picking of your guitar strings.

I hadn't known then who you were,
but recognized something in you
just the same, as you looked up
in your stocking cap, smiling
at us walking past, at ease with
playing in public anonymously.

Later, when I found out it was you
who had founded Windham Hill,
our seeing you all came together,
especially when I discovered
your New England Roads CD,
which we now mediate with

every morning, I realized that
it was you that we saw playing
as the snow fell deliberately,
by degrees, the same way
in which you pluck your strings,
delighting in the good Buddhism

of the moment and deepening
what is that is resonant,
lingering as snowflakes do
and the notes you play
in nourishing all those who
become present enough to listen.

ろ

Tall Firs

In memory of W. S. Merwin

       The evening I heard
that you passed
I looked out and watched

the long rays of twilight
touch the tops
of tall firs
across the field's expanse

and thought about
the first spring buds
I'd have to relearn
in order to remember their names.

I Went Back for My Father

I went back for my father
after calling him from a pay phone
in Chinatown on Christmas eve.
The call threw him into a muddle,

making me aware that being
on the phone confused him,
that he didn't know where I was
which made it difficult to know

where he was and what he was doing.
I went back for my father,
after hitchhiking to Stinson Beach,
after reading at a jazz club in San Anselmo,

after going to a festival on top
of Mount Tamalpais and being exposed
to all that nakedness in the California sun.
I went back for my father

who taught himself to read and write
using a Polish-English dictionary,
who immigrated from Eastern Europe
just before Hitler invaded Poland,

who was wounded in France when he batted
away a grenade a German soldier threw
and saved his squad, who carried shrapnel
in his right shoulder for the rest of his life,

his purple heart laid away in a drawer.
I went back for my father
and saw him surrounded by mental patients
in a locked ward of the soldier's home,

some patients rocking back and forth
in restraints, some stared stolidly into
nothingness, one wore a torn straw hat.
My father sat silently in a wheelchair in the sun.

I could neither weep nor speak because he was
beyond help and no longer recognized me.
I went back for my father
and after he died six years later when I received

the phone call I finally wept
not so much that he had died but for how he had
spent his last years, secluded in a nether world,
one I couldn't enter, one he couldn't leave.

Cara Cara

You are the champagne
of oranges. In making a fruit plate
for lunch, once I sliced
through you it was apparent

that you were different from
your brethren, glistening a deeper
hue, seedless, your segments
cleanly separated from the rind,

hardly having any pith. Your origin
is said to have been as a mutation,
spontaneously evolving
from a Washington navel orange tree,

but however you have arrived
to make your presence known
in the world of fruit,
you have done so with style

and taste, which has been described
as blackberry, cherry, and rose—
enhancing the palate to dance
and inspiring me to add

you along the dish that I named
The Carmen Miranda, since
you made the apple, banana,
blueberry, and strawberry slices

aware that they had rhythm,
that they became a constellation
of fruit because of you,
and made me think of the fruit hat

Carmen Miranda was known
for wearing when she sambaed,
but it was your blended
complex taste that made us

say, *Oh, I've never tasted*
anything as good as that before,
which makes you so distinct,
so special, such a delight,

in our savoring your essence,
that you tempt us into
whispering the delectable syllables
of your name into our lover's ears.

The Calling

In memory of Rainer Maria Rilke

When you called out
to your women, they responded
by vanishing somewhere
into another life.

The alchemy of their femininity
a deep mystery
they entered
and you with them,

augmented forever
by vanishing somewhere
into that other life,
but more so reappearing there

as if they traveled, bodily,
in taking flight,
on one level, but also in actuality,
moving beyond metaphor

into the metaphysics
of the spiritual, by calling out
to them in the first place,
as the angel announced to you

the initial lines of the First Elegy
at Duino, the castle owned
by Princess Maria Thurn und Taxis,
with whom you found nourishment

overlooking the Gulf of Trieste,
who also wrote the Kaiser
shortly after war broke out
to spare you from the slaughter

at the front, due to the enormity
of your contribution to literature;
how that maternal love
called to you, guiding you;

how also carnal love called to you,
providing to you; as did
Baladine Klossowska, your last lover,
whom you referred to

in the familiar as "Merline,"
who returned your call
by alternately standing by you
then giving you the space required

for the depths of your solitude
at the Chateau de Muzot,
overlooking the mists of the Rhone Valley
near Veyras, in Switzerland,

where you finished the outpouring
of the elegies and the unexpected
gift of the *Orpheus Sonnets*,
the woman who buoyed you

for that sole purpose
of precipitating the great wheels
of those soul movements,
producing those torrents of words

as if you brought them down
from those surrounding mountains
like sacraments written
on sacred stone tablets;

but it was always in the calling out
to your women and the response
of their calling back to you,
Rainer, Rainer, as an angel would,

that moved your life in so many ways
like a river and all of its tributaries,
their responses to the calling
leading them to vanish with you into

another life, wondering how far your
life might reach, and where night began,
upon which, as you wrote,
to work is to live without dying.

Of Angels

for Art Beck

Angels aren't really lost as much as they are
the enablers of our best intentions. There
may be lost angels, but they certainly aren't

emblematic or metaphorical of your poems.
Your poems are lyrical necessities, imagistic
works of art, always positing a philosophical

tautology. Angels are the enablers.
Your poems enable the angels to touch us
through our reading of them. Angels are

our touchstones to our better, or best, selves,
a kind of sanctity within a secular age,
inveterate in its crassness and turbidity.

Whereas, your poems, as angels, in a sense,
empower us to see, as Emily Dickinson wrote,
"at a slant," or at a different angle (a variant

of "angel"), leading to our experiencing insights,
which are, indeed, turns of the magnificent,
through your visons—*of angels.*

Saturday Afternoon, Ansonia

Sixty years ago this winter
I am still eight years old, grieving
the death of my mother.

The melee of children
teeming around me could be
a tableau from a painting by Brueghel.

We are awaiting our turns
on a toboggan run in the open field
across the street from the railroad flats.

The children are mostly
Catholic school chums, intoxicated
with the freedom of Saturday afternoon,

and they have a tendency of running wild,
not unlike Gorky's ragamuffins
descending upon the streets of Petersburg;

but this is Ansonia, a Connecticut milltown,
where my grandmother prepares
gwumpki that she will serve for dinner

by rolling hamburger and cooked rice
into cabbage leaves, then stacking each one
into an oval baking pan,

and submerging them with crushed tomatoes.
My father is working overtime
and will return after I do, if I am lucky,

since he doesn't want me out with the boys
because he believes I will hurt myself,
as I do, on the last run down the icy slope

by battering my right ankle against a stone
sticking above the snow crust, the one I sprain
and on which I will need to limp back home

where my father will take off his belt
to my grandmother's protestations in Polish
and beat me like he is whipping a dog,

the fragrance of ground beef and cabbage
permeating the air in the flat's warmth,
the glow of lamplight filtering through

a slit beneath the bedroom door,
the clock's loud ticking counting out
the lashes spoiling each second of oblivion.

Thinking about Johnny

Holding the corner
of the white wool ornamental blanket
you design to fold
with excruciating precision
into a rose-patterned coverlet,
I jest that this reminds me
of being sent into a corner
by one of the nuns when I was
in grammar school, although

I was never given that disciplinary
rigor, which led me to think
about Johnny, who would brazenly
tease a girl in the schoolyard
and then kiss her, which provoked
her breaking into tears, and then
her running back into class, where
the stern Polish nun would call
Johnny up to the head of the room.

She would then tear into him,
always a strand of his greased hair
falling rebelliously onto his forehead,
lips slightly opened in an impudent
pout, whereupon the nun would
set up the dressing screen, and order
Johnny to come behind it, where
all of us in class could hear
the straightedged ruler come down

onto Johnny's posterior, propelling
every child in the room to feel
the chill of icy terror, the humiliation
that Johnny never seemed to experience,
emerging from behind the screen
after the punishment had been dispensed,
cockier than ever, his bottom lip
quivering with indignant anger,
the bounce in his step haughtier, more
arrogant, the dangling strand of hair

a pendulum swinging one way
then another. And in the very rear
of the room, I sat with my head tilted
down behind a desk, next to Helen,
whom my Polish father would probably
have called stocky, where we might have
traded fugitive glances, shyly smiling,
momentarily, and not for the entire year
ever speaking a single word to each other.

The Farm

What held my attention at first
the most on that visit
to my parents' friends in rural

Florida was the enormity
of the hog, penned in with her
piglets, spattered with grime,

how she snorted, then the weight
of her wiggled, shuddering
in her ferocity, while I peered

through the slats in the wooden
boards, appraising their solidity
against the leaning massive

heft of hog. I must have been
five and the tableau of mud
and pigs didn't so much attract me

as I was transfixed in its amazement,
the sheer fascination of what
was wild in nature, even agrarian

husbandry, enrapt me by its vividness
and presence, enough so that
when I was brought back in to

the safety of the parlor, my hands
shook when I was asked to hold
the glass ball, portraying a snowfall

in New England, when it was shaken,
so much so that I dropped
its delicate shape and stature

whereupon it landed quietly on the soft
plushness of the carpet, surprising me
that it should break into pieces

despite it falling as lightly as it fell,
triggering my unabashed chagrin,
which summoned that it was time

for the visit to end, even though
apologies were offered and received
with decorum, that still had

my mother musing that the rides out
to the farm were to my benefit
and the psychic that she was

looked into the distance in her vision
of the future, seeing my inspiration
among farm animals amid their landscapes,

even the ones that might fall out
of my cupped hands, and in that
I might live a life of the imagination.

Amor Caritas

—in the grotto at Saint Gaudens, Cornish, New Hampshire

Before deep purple
water lilies floating in a marbled
pool decorated with fountains,

spouting from two gilt tortoises
on either end,
you rise perpetually in splendor.

Amor Caritas, gilded angel
of endearment and largesse, holding
a tablet over the garlands

woven around the top of your head,
wings and wingtips
reaching upward in an arc above

your shoulders to touch both ends
of the tablet you balance
perfectly and uphold such universal

tropes as peace, devotion to
divinity, good will, evident in your
name, *love* and *charity.*

A sash of passionflowers
girds your waist, a cincture for your
streaming pleated gown;

the visage of your face distinctly
womanly in its neither being male or
female, in its invitation to allow

our eyes to linger on the entirety of you
gleaming in gilt,
dazzling in the sunlight; your presence

alit without and within
in an undeniable strength and a purity;
the shimmer of your bronzed elegance

insisting what your angelic radiance
commands in offering that grace
itself is transcendence taking wing.

4

The Feather

My father bought me a hat
after my mother died.
The hat had a father on the side
of the band around the brim.
The feather was green and blue
and looked like just a wisp from
an underwing of a parakeet.
I would stroke it carefully,
missing my mother. I wore
the hat once a week for church,
and walked beside my father,
wearing his black arm band.
When I wore the hat it felt
like I was putting on my grief,
exposing my pain to the world,
that emerald and sky-blue feather,
enabling me to give it a semblance
of a name, whose submerged point
curled sharply within the felt,
glued in with a powerful mucilage,
and would prick my finger
whenever I tried to dislodge it.

Rose of Sharon

Hibiscus syriacas
"a kind of crocus growing as a lily among the brambles"
        —*Harper's Bible Dictionary*

The distinctive mauve of your petals
is reminiscent of the color
of a courtesan's lipstick,
the shade of which makes a tawdry
drunkard stumble, five petals

of dark pink, almost purple, forming
around an enlarged pistil
in the very center of your flower.
Your bloom is prolific
from May through September.

You are lavish, even lovely,
your color appears to suggest beauty
must go astray to proliferate
so much so as you do
since you usually bloom at night,

to think of you doing so
in the sheerness of moonlight
is to intimate you are a result
of a tryst with the best
of yourself and your shadow

that is not unlike ourselves
on our better days. By morning
you are only more promiscuous
by daylight, your preponderant
blossoms tipped cups brimming

with dew, reinvigorating
our imagination of your sustained
rose flush implies that your shade
is not only a color to savor but
also by drinking it in we come

to know the headiness of the taste
of your uncommon wine that
comes of age in our fields, and
whose branches announce you
by bending halfway to the ground,

making you appear to be the tree
of languishing kisses, whose
flowers resemble puckered lips
awaiting to be kissed.

Washing the Stones

What was explained to me
was that we were washing the stones

beside the reeds
in the pool along the river

because they didn't just represent
but actually were moments of our lives.

How the angel showed me
the way to cleanse the crystals,

precisely how to immerse our hands
into the swirling flow of the current,

the various colors of the jewels
sparkling in the water, as we rinsed

and rinsed them again, our hands
catching them in the streaming flow

of the river, a brisk wind
blowing the cattails we crouched amid,

rocking them stiffly above our heads.
What was instilled in me

was her kindness, how eloquent
her silent language was, how efficient

she was in teaching me to tend to process,
that it was something to persevere in

coming to know, how she pulled back
her hair in a bun above her tunic,

how everything about her emanated
tenderness in her acts of devotion, how

that was transferred to me through her,
washing and washing the precious stones

beneath the rippling water of the pool,
as we focused our eyes downward

in performing the work at hand,
although somehow seeing everything

around us at the same time, not once
ever revealing the beauty of her face,

which may have been too radiant for me
to be able to see without shielding my eyes.

Daniel Chester French's Standing Lincoln

Stockbridge, Massachusetts

Standing on your plinth
you appear to be greeting us
at the edge of the thick Berkshire woods
well behind the sculptor's studio.
But it is the gravity
that you summon from
the very lightness of the air
that forces us to straighten
our backs, to consider
all that you shouldered
with troubled sadness, the fraught
reverence of your clasped hands.

Meeting you
in this natural church amid the birches
and their windy shadows
brings us in accord with you
as we just begin
to feel your depths, the sorrows
combined with the compassion
to free the enslaved,
the dogged perseverance
to see the country through the war.
What heavy diligence
you made lighter by your anecdote, your wit

that belies your steady
disarming gaze.
Anyone looking up
at you who has anything
to be ashamed of will flinch
meeting your unblinking scrutiny.
Anyone who believes in goodness
and nurtures aspiration will be
lifted by your visage, alit
by the sunlight glinting through
the pines towering over
your brooding quietude.

Visitant

My favorite time is the morning,
when I fill the birdbath for the day
as I place the galvanized bucket
beneath the tap, or if I'm lucky
use the rainwater that's filled it
from the previous night's storm,
so I can flush out what detritus
remains from the rogue starlings
or a lone grackle that flutters
most of the water over the ground.

Another visitor is the bluebird,
the one who is more of a visitant
and a friend, who has hovered
by the kitchen window to announce
its presence, who stands erect
on the back of a garden chair,
appraising how clean the water
in the birdbath might be, who darts
to the rim and looks in, casting
its gaze over the pool's surface,

sipping as it meets its reflection,
before it flies up into the hazelnut tree,
and with its rufous breast and chalk-blue
feathers. streaks the air with color.

As They Pass

They make me look up.
There is a joy, brief as it is,
in seeing them row the air
but it is their voices which
greet us, such insistence
in their trumpeting, as they
fly overhead, passing quickly
not unlike our time here,
reminding us another season
is gone, another year soon
coming to a close, their rapid
strokes creaking above us
in their descent to the pond
where they will rest
in the water they will ripple,
mist rising above multicolored
leaves, streaking the woods gold,
the crimson of initial letters
that decorate old books, the wind
turning the pages as the geese
liberate what we think
as their mournful calls but actually
it is their voices that affirm
life as they pass through
its inscrutable mystery.

Anchorite

for Michael Miller

To find you in your realm,
not noticing I slipped through
the front door you left open
a crack, bringing bags of groceries
because you couldn't go out,
because you had fallen and were
healing, my being careful not to
crinkle the paper bags to alert you
of my entry into your apartment.
You are revealed to me in
the heat of composition, making
your marks on a yellow pad,
smiling comtemplatively, a faint
glow around your face, exhibiting
deep quiet as you ply your trade
of making poems, as I accomplish
crossing your threshold to place
the bags of groceries on
the counter of your galley kitchen.
I am grateful to have seen you
in your true element, the practice
of poetry leading you to
your many layered solitude,
an anchorite annotating margins
in an illuminated manuscript,
drawing up the initial letters
to each verse of your poems
with their taut lines, scrubbed
of any extra verbiage, their intent
to portray the rhythms of life
in all of their fullness, opening
both the mind and the heart
with the pure strokes of your pen.

Meditation, Basement, Yale Divinity School Chapel

More than fifty years ago,
and I still think of it, practicing
zazen with my mentors
in the circular basement
cloistered within the chapel,
how I saw the face of Christ
that appeared to me on the stone
blocks of the wall I focused
my attention on, how later I asked
if incense were being burned,
how on both occasions, the answer
was "no, not this time," knowing
full well I was still inhaling
a sweetness, how these decades
later I revisit those moments
of silence and shared solitude
with a group of others meditating,
how to this day what I rediscover
is the solace found amid the cold
stones of the chapel basement,
the delineation of the face
of divinity I can still see,
while inhaling an otherworldly
fragrance, which remains,
and whose scent continues to
accompany me along life's journey.

The Last Day

Marked by the pedestrian,
the unremarkable, the last day
will seem unassuming, benign.
The last day will neither
be buried in a blizzard nor
rage in wildfire but be more
like the winter fields during
January thaw, stretching into
boorishness and shades of brown.
The last day will be uneventful.
Neil at the post office won't
recall the last time he's seen you,
however, the staff at the Tailgate
will know you've not been around.
You won't be as dramatic as
your mother was, when you were
eight, and she collapsed from
a cerebral hemorrhage in
the bathroom and hit her head
on her way down against
the lip of the tub, nor will you
be gripped with a massive
heart attack like Zhivago, falling
to the pavement beneath
the tram lines in Moscow.
The sky for you on the last day
will neither be cloudy nor blue,
nor will you believe you might
be inhaling the fragrance
of souls from the spirit world
as Yeats did when a beautiful
woman passed his table from
behind, leaving a trail
of expensive perfume.
But when you decide to lay your

body down for your afternoon nap
on the last day, you may begin
to fall asleep, ticking off a list
of things to do, before going under,
possibly resolving the mystery
to wherever it is you will go,
before never rising again.

Acknowledgments

Grateful acknowledgment is made to the following publications where the following poems initially appeared, often in an earlier version.

The Arlington Literary Journal: "Taking Care of the Horses"

The Bluebird Word: "After the Blizzard"

The Comstock Review: "Green Heron"

Deep Wild Journal: Writing from the Backcountry: "November, Migration," "This Morning"

The Deronda Review (Special Soul Issue): "Washing the Stones" (as "Dream Angel")

Haight Ashbury Literary Journal: "Golden at the Trough"

Humana Obscura: "Tall Firs"

Michigan State University Libraries/*Short Edition:* "Redtail atop the Larch"

New World Writing: "An Offering of Grace," "Blue Evening: *for Doug Brown,*" "Finding the River Within," "I Went Back for My Father," "Rose of Sharon," "Saturday Afternoon, Ansonia"
Pensive: A Global Journal of Spirituality & the Arts: "Good Buddhism"

Porlock: "Discovering What to Say"

Quabbin Uniquely: "Black Bear Cub Crossing the Road"

The RavensPerch: Adding Breath to Words: "Button Box," "The Calling," "Carrying the Stone Buddha," "Creche," "Daniel Chester French's Standing Lincoln," "Manacled," "Thinking about Johnny"

The Seventh Quarry Poetry Magazine (Wales): "*Of Angels*"

Sho Poetry Journal (#3, "Revival Issue, Summer 2023): "The Farm"
Still Point Arts Quarterly (Special Themed Issue: *Immersed in Books*):
"Sam Murray, Bookseller"

Stone Poetry Quarterly: "Amor Caritas," "Baccarat Angel"

Tipton Poetry Review: "Discovering What to Say," Looking at Putin," Visitant"

"Green Heron" was nominated for a Pushcart Prize by the editors of *The Comstock Review.*

"November, Migration" was nominated for a Pushcart Prize by the editors of *Deep Wild: Writing from the Backcountry.*

"Redtail atop the Larch" was selected for Michigan State University Library's themed call for work about "Water", as a "standalone," in coordination with Michigan State University Broad Art Museum's fall 2023 exhibition, "Flint is Family in Three Acts," featuring photography of Latoya Ruby Frazier.

"This Morning" was issued as a letterpress broadside, printed by Lisa Rappaport of Littoral Press, Richmond, California, September 2024.

"Washing the Stones" (as "Dream Angel") was collected in the anthology *Dream Poems* (Lamar University Literary Press, 2025).

About the Author

Wally Swist was born April 26, 1953, in New Haven, Connecticut. His intellectual life began in working in bookstores for nearly a decade in the Yale University community. During this time, he also was a regular contributor to the arts section of *The New Haven Advocate*. After moving to western Massachusetts, he continued as a bookseller and a bookstore manager, for more than twenty years, dealing in antiquarian, new, and used books.

A prolific writer, he has published more than forty of his own books and chapbooks of poetry and prose. Readings of his work are online at National Public Radio and *The Writer's Almanac* with Garrison Keillor. He's also written countless essays, written several translations, and won dozens of awards.